Overcome Anxiety in Relationships

How to Eliminate Negative Thinking, Jealousy, Attachment, and Couple Conflicts—Insecurity and Fear of Abandonment Often Cause Irreparable Damage Without Therapy

By Lilly Andrew

Table of Contents

Introduction

Have you ever suffered from an overwhelming sense of anxiety in a relationship? You're not alone. Most people have gone through some form of this at one time or another in a relationship.

The good news is that this anxiety is natural, and you can keep it in check with a couple of simple tips and tricks. These tips and tricks will help prevent anxiety from sabotaging your blossoming relationship and your everyday life.

In this book, we will cover the different types of relationship anxiety that are common in most people. Moreover, we will discuss its effects on our physical and mental health and the different ways of dealing with them.

This book isn't just for those who are in new relationships, though. It also contains several tips for long-term relationships or marriages that are looking for ways to rekindle the spark of their relationship and remove some of the stress and worry they have.

Relationship anxiety issues are prevalent not only in new relationships. Thus, this book also provides extensive detail on how to combat relationship anxiety in long-term relationships and marriages. It has put together the information needed to achieve healthier and happier relationships with your significant other.

Chapter 1: Anxiety in Relationships

Anxiety can occur even in the most solid of relationships. Even if you and your partner are madly in love, trust each other, and respect each other's boundaries, there is still a chance that anxiety will impact your relationship at some point.

Perhaps you have constant worries about whether the relationship will last, whether you are good enough for your partner, whether they are trustworthy, or whether they are the right person for you. These are all forms of relationship anxiety. Relationship anxiety covers anything from feelings of insecurity to worrying thoughts. They can crop up at any time in a relationship even if the relationship itself is going quite well.

In fact, in some cases, these feelings are more likely to arise when your affection for your partner grows. You may feel you have more to lose now than when the relationship first started and you weren't as heavily invested.

Overseeing Anxiety

If not tended to, anxiety can take hold of your life and quickly make it difficult for you to complete other daily tasks. If you let your anxiety consume you, it can seriously affect your health and wellbeing. To make sure you keep tabs on your anxiety levels, there are several different things you can do.

For starters, you can offer your services or help to others. This will give you a feeling of dependability. Many different charities need volunteers. Alternatively, you can simply just reach out to a new friend.

You can also make sure that you catch unnecessary worries early. Make sure you forgive yourself for having negative thoughts from time to time. These acts of self-love will take you one step closer to tackling your anxiety.

The Nature of Anxiety

Fear is one of the primary emotions, and pretty much all humans will experience it at one time or another. More people have relationship fears than you may think. Anxiety isn't exclusive to humans either. Studies have shown that all animal species also experience feelings of anxiety.

The human body has been set up to sense fear. This instinct has been used to keep humans alive. However, in our modern-day society where our lives are less at risk of death each day and threats have become significantly less imminent, this fear and anxiety manifest itself in different ways, such as in our work or relationships.

The Effects of Anxiety

The effects of anxiety on both your mental and physical health can be quite dangerous if they aren't dealt with. Some of the common symptoms include feeling tired, nervous, tense, or restless. You may also find yourself overwhelmed with a feeling of doom, panic, or danger hanging over you as you go about your everyday life. Aside from this, other effects of anxiety are an increase in your heart rate, trembling sensations, and sweating.

Another intriguing effect of anxiety is the inability to concentrate on anything. This is because your mind continually wanders to places of worry and concern, making everyday tasks challenging to complete.

The Causes of Anxiety

The root cause of anxiety differs from person to person. In truth, no one knows precisely what causes anxiety. However, several different factors are involved that ultimately lead to a state of anxiety. One of these includes past experiences or experiences from a young age. Painful experiences as a child, such as abuse, neglect, the loss of a parent, or bullying, can lead to anxiety in later life. Your current life situation can also cause anxiety. If you are out of work, have money issues, or have lost someone close to you, your anxiety levels may rise. Physical or mental health problems can also lead to anxiety—for example, when you are living with a serious illness or tackling a psychological issue such as depression.

The Management of Anxiety

Anxiety can be managed in different ways. One easy tactic to implement when struggling with anxiety is to take slow deep breaths. By deliberately slowing down your breath, you lower your heart rates, helping you reduce anxiety.

One of the worst aspects of anxiety is when you overthink terrible things that haven't occurred yet. Telling yourself to stay in the moment and live in the present will help you avoid these made-up scenarios. Another tactic is self-talk. Make sure you lay out what are facts and what you have created through anxiety. This will help you keep everything in check.

Depression With Anxiety and Relationship

Anxiety can lead to depression, which can greatly damage your relationship. Depression can lead to an unhappy state of mind. This can leave you having unwanted thoughts and acting negatively. If not dealt with properly (e.g., discussing it with your partner), ultimately, your depression can lead to more serious issues in your relationship.

One aspect of your relationship that can be affected by depression is you and your partner's sex life. Depression can complicate an intimate connection with your partner. Studies have shown that depression leads to a decrease in libido. When your sex life suffers, so does the relationship, as having a healthy sex life helps release stress and increase each other's trust.

Tips to Help Reduce Anxiety Levels Using Exercise

One way to defeat your levels of anxiety is through exercise. Many studies link exercise to a reduction in anxiety levels. Exercise is deemed vital in supporting mental health. It reduces stress, which is one of the critical components that contribute to anxiety. Exercise reduces fatigue, increases your concentration and brain function, and controls your anxiety levels.

There is a direct link between how your body feels and how your mind works. When you improve how your body feels through regular exercise, you will have a healthier mind. Chemicals in your brain often work as natural painkillers, which improve life aspects, such as sleep. This can significantly reduce the impact of anxiety.

Overseeing Stress and Building Solid Relationships

If you let it, stress can significantly impact relationships and ultimately lead to unhappy relationships or even a breakup. However, this doesn't have to be the case! You can use some tactics to overcome the feelings of stress and build a strong and stable base for an intimate relationship with your partner.

1. Don't be afraid to disagree. It's essential to have your own opinion on things. That doesn't mean you should argue for the sake of argument. However, make sure you continue to stand up for what you believe in.

2. Communicate. Talk—this is the most important aspect of any relationship, and unsurprisingly, it resolves most issues that couples experience. Continue to communicate how you feel with your partner and make sure you listen when they do the same.

3. Keep up other interests. It's always healthy to have interests outside of the relationship. It's good to have your friends, and you have to trust your partner when they do activities with their own set of friends.

Attraction Anxiety

Attraction anxiety occurs when you become so anxious in a relationship that your body goes into survival mode. At this point, you will find yourself becoming more attracted to people outside of the relationship, which, as you would expect, can cause a lot of issues.

Your body can have these feelings when you are anxious that your partner may be cheating on you or when you fear that they will leave you. Through this unnecessary fear of being alone, you may subconsciously seek out another mate on a primal level before you ever need to.

The Diamond Inside of Anxiety

The diamond inside of anxiety is an interesting concept and one to bear in mind when you are struggling to stay on top of your emotions. Ultimately, the concept states that underneath your anxiety issues, you have a great personality just waiting to come out, much like a diamond in the rough.

By taking steps to open up to your partner about any anxiety issues, breaking down those internal barriers, and becoming more trustworthy, you will ultimately leave yourself in a relationship that is stronger than ever and will only grow from there.

If the relationship doesn't work out for whatever reason, you will also be able to handle the issue of loss and be better prepared for another relationship when the time is right.

Undesirable Relationships Can Cause Anxiety and Stress

It's worth pointing out at this stage that not all relationships are supportive when it comes to dealing with anxiety and stress. Some bad relationships can lead to more anxiety, stress, and even serious health problems.

One of the main signs that you are in a bad relationship is when your partner is giving you reasons not to trust them. You may have previously been very trustworthy, but over time, behavior such as sneaking out, not coming home at night, or lying about where your partner is going can lead you to become more anxious and stressed.

Another sign of a bad relationship is the lack of communication. If your partner isn't opening up to you or providing you with reasonable reassurance about their feelings, then this can lead to you feeling more anxious about where you stand or where the relationship is going.

Performance Anxiety

Performance anxiety is the fear of being unable to perform. This can occur in relationships, as well as in music or sporting environments. In a relationship, performance anxiety occurs mainly in men when they are unable to become aroused and have sex with their partner. Performance anxiety occurs more frequently than you might think, but because it isn't spoken about openly, you may feel like you are the only person who is suffering. This can be due to a number of reasons. Some of which are health-related, while some are related to our mental health. If not discussed and resolved, this can lead to fractions in the relationship, which can, in turn, lead to even more performance issues. It's important to talk to your partner if this issue occurs to help them understand what may be causing it and allow them to support you to resolve the problem.

Tips for Overcoming Performance Anxiety

If you've ever experienced performance anxiety in a relationship, you will know it can feel embarrassing and doesn't go away without using some smart tips and tricks. Some tips to overcome performance anxiety in a relationship include the following:

- *Reduce your caffeine levels to lower the chance of a heightened heart rate.* This will prevent you from building up too much anxiety, allowing you to focus on the task at hand.
- *If you don't succeed at first, try again!* Just because you weren't able to perform once, it doesn't mean it will be an issue every time. Don't shy away from trying to have sex with your partner.
- *Focus on the positives rather than the negatives.* Think about what is you like about having sex with your partner rather than what could go wrong.
- *Act naturally and be yourself.* Performance anxiety really isn't uncommon in relationships. It's important you don't change yourself. Be honest to yourself.
- *Exercise and improve your diet.* Both of these will help any physical issues you may have that lead to performance anxiety in the bedroom.

All these tips will help you overcome performance anxiety in your relationship.

Trust and Anxiety

You will notice from reading this book that trust levels and the impact of anxiety go hand in hand. Doubting a relationship's integrity can be one of the primary sources of anxiety and stress. In the long run, it will have a very detrimental effect on your relationship.

It is not uncommon that people fall for their partners because of their fun lifestyle, packed with friends and social events. However, if they stop seeing their friends because you have trust issues and prevent them from hanging out with other people, you may end up less attracted to them as they no longer live the fun life they had when you met. Either that or your partner will become frustrated with you for not letting them live their life and end the relationship themselves.

What Can You Do About Relationship Anxiety?

So how can you tackle this relationship anxiety? Firstly, you need to allow yourself to trust that your partner is faithful to you until they show you otherwise. If there are no signs of them being unfaithful, then you need to trust them to live their life. This will also give you the time to go out and live your own life, so it's a win-win!

Having secure connections outside of the relationship gives both partners a stronger foundation for building their relationship. Moreover, when you know you have a strong group of friends and family to fall back on if needed, it puts you in a better position to be less stressed about the relationship potentially ending.

Another way to overcome relationship anxiety is to talk about it out loud with your partner. Saying it out loud takes the burden off your shoulders, allowing your partner to reassure you. You may even be surprised to learn that your partner may have the same issues as well!

Chapter 2: Eliminate Insecurity and Fear in Your Relationship

Relationship insecurities are extremely common, and most people have experienced being insecure at one time or another in their life. However, when these insecurities become chronic, it can severely damage your most intimate relationships and your everyday life.

Having severe relationship insecurities takes away your ability to be at peace. It will leave you on edge or inauthentic around your significant other. Interestingly, most relationship insecurities come from within rather than from how your partner acts or what they do.

These feelings are often ingrained from an early age, potentially from attachment issues with your parents or your family members. They could also manifest from being hurt in the past by a previous partner or from being rejected by someone you cared for deeply.

Most relationship fears come from irrational thoughts. Perhaps you may think that you are not good enough, that you will have nothing without your partner, that no one will truly love you, or that you will not ever find anyone else.

If any of this resonates with you, don't worry—we have pulled together some handy tips and tricks for you to help reduce these worries to a more manageable level.

A Relationship Based on Trust

To put it simply, healthy relationships don't exist without significant amounts of trust. However, almost all of us have experienced times in our lives when trust has been broken in a relationship, whether it be through something as small as a white lie or as big as cheating.

It is essential to make sure that these feelings of distrust in previous partners are not brought into a new relationship with a partner that has never given you a reason to distrust them.

Trust is hard to build up but very easy to knock down, so it's important to work consistently and repeatedly. You need to be open to trusting your partner until they give you reason not to.

Some of the significant ways to improve trust include the following:

- Communicating
- Thinking things through before making any decisions
- Being consistent with each other
- Honoring your commitments
- Listening actively
- Being honest
- Admitting mistakes
- Being open about your feelings

All these can be used to increase trust in a relationship, but it only works when both sides are willing to commit together. It is important to notice when a partner is making these efforts and attempt to meet them halfway.

Method to Overcome Fear of Abandonment

One of the most significant causes of anxiety in a relationship is the fear of being abandoned. This can come from previous relationship experience or from issues that stem from childhood.

Many people experience fears of abandonment. What's frustrating is that if you do suffer from this fear, it is only heightened further when you have genuinely fallen for your partner. The more you like them, the more you feel you have to lose!

This fear can be overcome, however, using a range of different tips and techniques. One of these is self-kindness. Accepting yourself for who you are and being warm and friendly to yourself will allow you to become a better friend to yourself, reducing the fear of being left alone.

Another technique is mindfulness. Being mindful prevents your imagination from running away with negative thoughts; instead, it keeps these in check with the help of positive self-talk.

Mindfulness consists of recognizing what these feelings are and then managing them with positive self-talk so that they disappear. It may work to ignore these thoughts in the short term, but they may become overwhelming further down the line.

Signs You Are Insecure in Your Relationship and How to Fix It

Now more than ever, with our access to social media, insecurity is rife in relationships. However, this doesn't mean that relationship insecurity should rule your life. There are things you can do to help resolve the issue. But before that, here are some signs that you are insecure in your relationship.

1. You want to look at your partner's phone. Your partner goes to have a shower and leaves their phone on the sofa. What do you do? If your initial reaction was to check it and see who they are talking to, you might be struggling with insecurity in your relationship. While it may seem innocent to you, it's a direct invasion of their privacy.

2. You don't like them having a social life. If you're worried about your partner meeting their friends in the park, this is a massive sign of mistrust and insecurity. If you can't let yourself be okay with your partner seeing friends without thinking they will cheat on you, then it's time to check your insecurities.

3. You avoid confrontation. We aren't suggesting that arguing all the time is good, but if you hold things in and don't discuss them, there will ultimately be a blow-up. One significant sign of insecurity is avoiding talking about anything confrontational when necessary for a successful intimate relationship.

Approaches to Let Go of Insecurity in Your Relationship

So how can you remove some of these insecurities and allow your relationship to grow and progress? Here are some simple approaches to life that will let go of some of your insecurities.

1. Remember that not everything is about you. First of all, it's essential to step back and realize that not everything is about you. If your partner doesn't want to go on a night out, it doesn't mean they don't want to be seen with you. It probably just means they're tired and don't want to go on a night out.

2. Don't feel paranoid over nothing. Girls have friends who are guys, and guys have friends who are girls. It is 2020, after all. Just because your partner has friends of the opposite sex, it doesn't mean they are cheating on you or that they are anything more than just the friends your partner tells you they are.

3. Don't avoid confrontation. Facing problems head-on and discussing them until they are resolved will develop a level of trust so firm you will feel comfortable talking anything and everything with your partner. In the long run, this is worth the initial tough conversations.

4. Stop being dependent on others. Self-love is the most important love. Having this in place before going out into the world of dating is vital if you want to have long and meaningful relationships. While having cuddles and kisses are lovely, it's vital to love yourself first and know you will be okay if these things ever go away.

The Effect of Insecurity

While you may feel that if you keep your insecurities to yourself and keep them from your partner, everything will be just fine, this is sadly far from the truth. Ultimately these feelings will filter through, whether through words or actions, and they will have several damaging effects on your relationship.

1. Trusting your significant other. The first and foremost of any successful relationship is trust. Trust is the cornerstone of any romantic relationship. Without fully trusting your partner, you can end up pushing them away, or struggle to open up emotionally, which will hinder the relationship's progression over time.

2. You turn negative thoughts into actions. Everyone has negative thoughts; that's a fact of life. However, if you continuously bombard yourself with negative thoughts, you will ultimately internalize them, which will then impact how you act. These actions will also have an overall negative effect on your relationship.

3. You require constant reassurance. Again, everyone requires some reassurance once in a while. However, if you need constant validation, then something is seriously wrong. Aside from this, when your partner gets tired of the constant need to reassure, this will lead to you becoming even more insecure. This type of behavior needs to be rectified fast.

How Might I Overcome Insecurity?

Now that we have established some of the crucial features of insecurity, let's discuss some of the easy tips and tricks you can use to overcome those negative thoughts and actions.

1. Improve your self-esteem. The practice of improving your self-esteem will go a long way to removing those insecurities in your relationship. By taking the time to do this, you will feel more confident and trustworthy. Examples of excellent practices for self-esteem include taking a personal day, going to a spa, or exercising more frequently.

2. Trust in your partner and yourself. Trust equals happiness, plain and simple. Healthy relationships are built on trust as it allows your partner to live their life and blossom. It's also essential to trust your instincts. If your significant other has never cheated or given you a reason to think they would, then why wouldn't you trust them?

3. Learn not to overthink. Finally, it's imperative not to overthink. If your partner is going to see some friends without you, don't take it personally. Overthinking these simple day-to-day human actions can lead to further questioning and distrust for absolutely no reason. It's important to note when you are doing this and to suppress this feeling immediately.

Try Not to Let Fear Destroy Your Relationship

A little bit of fear in a relationship is a good thing! The presence of fear of losing your significant other reinforces how strong your feelings are toward your partner. It also shows how much you care. However, having too much fear present in a relationship can ultimately sabotage it to the point of disrepair—but it doesn't have to.

One way of tackling your fears in a relationship is by communicating with your partner. By telling your partner of your worries, you are allowing them into your mind to give them a better understanding of how you work. You should also be there to listen to your partner's fears. You may even be surprised to find that they have many of the same concerns as you do!

There are also different types of fear, such as the fear of loneliness, the fear of boredom, and the fear of change, to name a few. It's essential to identify which fears are relevant to you as that will help you better combat them in the future.

By tackling your relationship fears as a team, you are taking the first steps to build trust and taking your relationship to the next level.

Adapting to Fear in Your Relationship

Now that you have successfully recognized what fears you have in your relationship, the work does not stop there. It is essential to keep a check on these fears. Make sure you discuss them where necessary. Keep a lid on them to prevent them from negatively impacting your relationship going forward.

By building a robust and trustworthy relationship base, you will feel comfortable calling each other out of actions or feelings that are stemmed by fear. This will allow you both to keep your fears in check while continuing to progress in your relationship.

Over time, these relationship fears will be quashed by a consistent positive action from the two of you. The fear will become less and less as the relationship progresses—but only if you can put these solid foundations in place initially.

Liken this to building a house. When building a house, you wouldn't start with the roof. You build the foundations first, then the walls and structure supports, and then the roof. You will know whether you have a strong and sturdy house only after the initial work on the foundation has been done.

Chapter 3: The Most Common Problems of Couples

Unsurprisingly, many married couples are faced with very similar issues, most of which can be resolved, avoided, or fixed.

1. Sexual differences: While some people feel uncomfortable saying it out loud, physical intimacy is vital for long-lasting relationships. Because of this, sexual differences and loss of libido are prevalent issues for married couples.

2. Beliefs and values: There will always be some differences in a marriage, and that is no bad thing. It is healthy to have debates and discussions on different topics. Unfortunately, however, some differences can be too much to simply ignore. These are often deemed as someone's beliefs or values. These can often be overlooked or ignored early in a relationship, but they can lead to major marital issues over time.

3. Stages of life: This topic is often overlooked when it comes to relationships, but the issue of life stages is prevalent, especially in our modern, fast-moving society. Sometimes the source of marital issues occurs from partners simply wanting different things out of life. These issues are more common in relationships between partners who have a significant age gap.

4. Stress: This one occurs in pretty much every marriage at least once. Stress can be caused by several different things, such as family, mental health, or financial issues. How this stress is handled can determine how significant this issue can be in a marriage.

Issues That Threaten Even Happy Marriages

Issues aren't just reserved for those in unhappy marriages; there are also issues that can plague even the best of marriages. However, the difference between good and bad marriages is how these issues are tackled and how much each partner allows the problem to escalate before tackling it. One issue that often rears its ugly head even in a happy marriage is overstepping boundaries.

Studies have shown that once a couple has married, it isn't uncommon for a spouse to change their significant other. This could be anything from their values to what they wear—the spouse tries to change their partner.

These attempts can lead to issues between the couple that can become damaging if not dealt with. Infidelity can also be present in a happy marriage in the form of emotional cheating. So while there may be no cheating, emotional infidelity can occur when two people drift apart and begin connecting with people outside of the marriage.

Sometimes it's good to know that even those in happy marriages will suffer issues in their relationship. This can help put your anxiety over your relationship into perspective and allow you to be a little less hard on yourself.

Mistakes in a Relationship

Everybody makes mistakes in relationships, especially in long-term relationships. It is unfair to expect that neither you nor your partner will ever make any relationship mistakes. Holding an unreasonable standard such as this can lead to unnecessary pressure being put on a relationship, which leads to different issues entirely.

Mistakes can vary in how significant they are. Some can be rectified over time and with discussions, and some are tough to come back from. One common relationship mistake is taking your partner for granted. As a relationship grows and develops, it can be easy to settle into a new life norm.

All that is well and good. However, it can sometimes lead to partners becoming too comfortable, and they begin to take their significant other for granted. Dropping your privacy walls is another mistake some people make as relationships go on.

Initially, a close relationship is formed by keeping each other's best-kept secrets and becoming a reliable source of trust for your partner. However, if these secrets slip out to close friends and family over time, it can lead to new issues of trust and anxiety coming into the relationship as a result.

Battling About Money

As a relationship grows, your lives become more intertwined than ever. This is a great thing as it integrates each partner into each other's lives, sharing more memories. These memories include taking trips together, having pets, buying cars, or even owning a house. All of these steps are important and significant for a relationship, but with it brings their issues surrounding finances.

Sometimes issues can arise from the overspending habits of a particular partner. You may become uncomfortable with how much they spend on things such as clothes, shoes, or other items that you do not deem necessary. To better understand each other and find a form of compromise, it is essential to discuss why you feel this way and why your partner feels differently.

Another issue that can arise in a relationship surrounding money is regarding saving money. You may have different ideas on how much you should be saving each week, which can lead to disagreements on how you want to go about saving money.

Again, it is essential to discuss these issues to help gain a perspective of what your partner is thinking and why they feel different to you about saving. You will then be able to set common savings goals that hopefully meet both parties' needs.

Determinedly Defending One's Point of View

Standing up for what you believe in is vitally important in any relationship. If you don't stick by your morals and beliefs just to keep your partner happy and avoid confrontation, you will ultimately end up sad and anxious about the relationship.

Someone's point of view and beliefs are a massive part of what makes each of us individually. It is also likely one of the main reasons that your partner fell for you in the first place. Therefore, it is good to know how to stand up for yourself without coming across as defensive to help keep your points of view intact.

When discussing your point of view on a topic, make sure you have done your research. When you pitch a thought, there will be those who agree with you, but there will also always be those who disagree with you.

Also, make sure that you are susceptible to constructive criticism. It is one thing to welcome it verbally. However, by also showing you are taking it on board, you are letting your partner know that you are willing to listen and learn and that they should be doing the same.

Having a strong point of view also requires a lot of patience. It may be that your partner simply does not get it at first, and that's okay. Be prepared to stick with your guns, and over time, they will realize just how vital that particular topic is to you.

Problems That Lead to a Marriage in Crisis—Avoid Them at All Cost!

"Crisis" is a big word and one to only be used when necessary! Therefore, it's vital to tackle these potential issues before they turn into a crisis that may lead to divorce.

1. Losing libido: There's no point in pretending that sex is not a large part of any relationship. Over time, your sex life in marriage can wane if you allow it. Therefore, it is necessary to maintain a healthy sex life with your partner. Communicate your likes and dislikes. Continue making your partner feel desired through actions and words.

2. Emotional or physical cheating: Both emotional and physical cheating is hard to come back from if left unresolved. Physically cheating on someone is a step that, in some cases, is impossible to resolve, and it can lead to divorce in some cases. Moreover, discovering that your partner has emotionally or physically cheated on you can lead to newfound levels of stress and anxiety issues as a result.

3. Money disputes: Another issue that can arise from marriage is money disputes. These can come from several reasons, such as how money is spent or how money is saved. These disputes can begin small at first, but if they aren't discussed in detail, this can lead to further resentment down the line.

Two Hidden Sexual Problems Between Couples

Ultimately, issues between couples with regard to sexual problems come down to two main points. These two problems are more common than you might think, and how you deal with them as a couple is the most important aspect of helping the relationship to continue to grow and prosper.

Firstly, there is often one partner who is disgruntled with how much sex is in the relationship. This may be a partner who wishes they have more sex as a couple, or this may be a partner who wishes they are less frequently making love. Without being communicated about, this frustration may lead to further resentment over time.

This can be an issue that trickles over into other parts of the relationship, so it's important to stop these issues in their tracks through early communication. It will allow partners to better understand each other before progressing with the relationship. This brings us onto our second point, which is communication. Couples often struggle to discuss what they enjoy in the bedroom and what they don't like.

This can sometimes lead to a less enjoyable and less intimate experience in the bedroom, which will potentially stunt the progression of the overall relationship.

Questions and Problems That Couples Have

1. How do I know they're the one?

It can be difficult sometimes to know whether someone is "the one" for you. Frustratingly, some friends make it seem so obvious with their partner that it begins to make your question your feelings. Always remember that everyone has different feelings, and it is impossible to compare your relationship to another. Therefore, it is hard to tell if someone is the one. However, if you enjoy spending time together and picture a future with your partner, that is usually a good sign.

2. I'm not ready to get married, but my partner is.

This is quite common and, when you think about it, makes a lot of sense. Realistically, what are the chances that you and your partner will both be in the same emotional place at the same time? If your partner is the right person for you, they will respect your position and wait patiently for you to become ready in your own time.

3. I feel like my partner doesn't trust me.

This can be a tricky one and needs to be dealt with delicately. Firstly, it's worth addressing this feeling with your partner, explaining why you feel this way. This will allow your partner to discuss why they may not trust you or why they don't want to change their behavior. It will give you a starting point when you need to adjust your relationship accordingly.

Chapter 4: A Healthy Relationship Without Jealousy

Start trusting your partner and stop negative thinking and jealousy. Jealousy can often be perceived as a sign of love, but this isn't the case. While some may feel that jealousy comes from a deeply rooted effect for their significant other, studies have attributed it to other traits such as low self-esteem, feelings of possessiveness and insecurity, dependency on others, and feelings of inadequacy.

Jealousy can only be resolved by accepting that this is the case and working on yourself. Working on your inner confidence will alleviate some of the jealousy that you feel toward your partner. This will ultimately help you remove any aspects of insecurity or dependency on others so that you feel adequate and suitable as a partner.

It is also important to communicate these feelings of jealousy to your partner and not keep them to yourself. How you communicate these feelings is very important. You shouldn't approach it with anger; you should address the issues with an understanding that your behavior isn't right and you need to change.

By doing this, your partner will better understand the root of your jealousy and appreciate that you are working to improve these feelings. In turn, they are likely to adjust their behaviors to help you become more confident.

Extraordinary Steps to Overcome Possessiveness and Jealousy

1. Leave the past in the past. Perhaps you have been lied to or cheated by a previous partner. Maybe you have abandonment issues from childhood events. These past events need to be put to one side when starting a new relationship. Bringing any of your emotional baggage into a new relationship will make you doubt your partner or stay closed off when, in reality, they have done nothing to deserve this type of behavior toward them.

2. Have your own life. Make sure that you build up your hobbies and social circles before starting any relationship. It is not up to your significant partner to keep you occupied or provide entertainment to your life. Having these external interests will make you feel less jealous when they do similar activities with their friends.

3. Meet their friends. Another way to reduce the feelings of jealousy is to make an effort to meet and befriend your partner's friends. By getting to know them and watching your partner interact with them, you will see nothing to worry about and begin to feel more comfortable about them spending more time with their friends when you aren't around.

Vanquishing Jealousy in Your Relationship

As you may have gathered, you must remove the concept of jealousy from your relationship to grow and develop over time. Removing jealousy from your relationship will allow both you and your partner to feel more comfortable in each other's presence. It will also lead to a healthier and more positive relationship in the long run.

Without jealousy, you will be able to trust each other's actions completely until they do anything to make you feel otherwise. Moreover, you will both go on to have fun, wholesome lives that include each other but also have value without each other as well. Vanquishing jealousy from your relationship will open up whole new doors in your relationship you didn't know were possible.

Anger and Jealousy: Dealing with Anger at an Ex

Being betrayed by an ex-partner can be very damaging to any future relationships if you don't take the time to deal with these issues directly. It may be that you have seen a picture of them and look extremely happy even after hurting your feelings. This can make the feelings of anger and jealousy pop up, and these need to be addressed to ensure they don't impact your relationships.

The first step is to acknowledge that you have these emotions. They are perfectly normal, and most people get them. These emotions can arise even after you no longer have attraction feelings toward them anymore.

Once you have acknowledged these emotions, it is time to express them healthily. One easy way to do this is by writing down how you feel on a piece of paper before ripping it up and throwing it away. This allows the thoughts to come out of your head before ceremonially throwing them into the trash and moving on with your life.

Recuperating After Infidelity: Steps to Rid Yourself of Negative Feeling and Self-Doubt

One of the most difficult relationship issues to come back from is infidelity. Even if this occurred many years ago in a different relationship, it could still be difficult to shake the impact of this in relationships years later. Don't worry, though—there are steps that you can take to remove the feelings of self-doubt from your mind.

1. Act fast. When you start to notice the feelings of trust issues, anxiety, and fear rearing their ugly heads, act immediately. Don't allow these feelings to manifest themselves. Reassure yourself with positive self-talk and remind yourself that there is no need to have these feelings in your current relationship.

2. Leave the past in the past. While it can be very difficult to do at first, you have to leave your past in the past. Your previous partner may have broken your trust before, but it isn't fair to put those same feelings onto your current partner, especially if they haven't acted in any way that would lead you to feel that way. It's important to remind yourself that these are issues of the past and not ones you need to worry about anymore.

3. Talk about your feelings. It can also be extremely helpful to discuss your feelings with others, ideally your current partner. Opening up to them and allowing yourself to be vulnerable will help your partner to better understand you and potentially alter their behavior to help meet you halfway.

4. Don't compare. This is an important one! Don't compare your current partner to any previous partners. It is unfair to your current relationship to compare the two. Treat each relationship as its entity. Act and react accordingly rather than on previous experiences.

5. Write down your thoughts. It can also be beneficial to write down how you are feeling. Sometimes writing down how you feel can show you just how silly you are being. This tactic also allows you to release some of these negative thoughts from being trapped in your mind.

6. Keep in mind that not everything is about you. It might be hard to believe, but the whole world doesn't revolve around you! When experiencing negative thoughts, it's easy to think that way. However, it's important to remember that your partner spends time with friends and family not because they don't want to spend time with you but because they want to spend time with those people.

7. See your setbacks as temporary. Don't beat yourself up if you fall back into bad habits from time to time. Setbacks are temporary and all part of the learning curve as you grow into a more positive person and a more supportive partner.

8. Engage in positive self-talk. Changing your inner dialogue with positive talk is a great way to help you crush old ingrained negative thoughts.

The Awesome Power of Positive Thinking

Thinking positively and having optimism can have an incredible impact on your life. You'll be amazed at what you can achieve when you can maintain positive thoughts. A positive person finds good in even the worst situations. They also assume the best in people until they prove otherwise. This is great when it comes to letting your anger towards an ex-partner go.

Instead of thinking about how they wronged you or how angry they made you, you should focus on all the positives that came out of dating them, no matter how small. Maybe you made some new friends by dating them, took up a new hobby, or went to an event you would never have been before dating them.

If nothing else, the experience of dating them has helped mold you into the person you are today. It also teaches you what you are and aren't looking for in a partner in the future.

Positive Thinking and How It Can Help You Overcome Fear

One of the most powerful ways to overcome fear is by practicing the idea of positive thinking. Positive thoughts will help keep you optimistic and prevent negative thoughts from dictating your actions. If you allow it, fear can run rife in your mind, making you more anxious and worked up when, in most cases, there is no reason to do so!

By being positive and thinking positive thoughts, you will stifle any negative thoughts before they manifest themselves and turn into bigger issues, such as anxiety or fear.

You can practice positive thinking by writing down any current negative thoughts and flipping them around to being more positive. This will help you tackle those negative thoughts when they arise in the future, which will allow you to become a more positive person going forward.

Approaches to Overcome Jealousy

Jealousy is prevalent in some form in many different relationships. When you care deeply for someone, it is natural to want to spend time with them and know that they feel the same way as you do.

Having strong feelings for someone does not mean it is okay to feel jealous when they spend time with others without you, especially if they are your partner's close friends or family. To make sure you keep your jealousy in check, it is important to note when you are starting to feel these feelings.

If your partner has a lot of friends outside of the relationship, that's great! It's not up to them to keep you entertained, so it's important that you have your social circles and hobbies so that you aren't so dependent on your partner.

Mesmerizing to Stop Feeling of Jealousy

Another less common tactic for removing the feeling of jealousy from your relationship is through hypnosis. Mesmerizing yourself with positive self-talk and triggers that reduce the feelings of jealousy will greatly improve your relationship and your feelings of self-worth.

Hypnosis is a good tool for jealousy traits that have been around for some years and are heavily embedded in your psyche. Hypnosis focuses on the root cause of your jealousy; this is an extremely effective tool for removing jealousy from your relationship.

Bad Thinking Habits and How to Fix Them

1. Make time for negative thoughts.

Instead of running from your emotions, you should take the time to address these feelings in a structured and manageable way. It's important to set aside some specific time to address these feelings. Allow yourself to understand them better, and to try to move on from them in the future. If not, these negative thoughts will continue to come and go, making it difficult for you to move past them and progress in your life and relationships.

2. Swap out negative thoughts.

Now that you have put some time in your calendar to address these negative thinking habits, it's time to work on replacing them with some more positive thoughts! By sitting down and coming to the root cause of these negative thoughts, you can begin to evaluate these thoughts and understand why you have them. You will then be able to replace them with positive thoughts.

For example, your partner is going to hang out with friends, and being a negative thinker, you instantly conclude that your partner would rather spend time with their friends than you. If you take time to evaluate this negative thought, you will be able to change it to something positive—for example, being proud of your partner for having close friends and a great social life.

3. Become your own best friend.

The easiest person to befriend is yourself! By becoming your own best friend, you will no longer rely on other people to keep you entertained. One of the main issues of anxiety crops up from being so dependent on your partner to have fun or to be entertained. By practicing the art of self-love and becoming your own best friend, you will become much more comfortable in your own company and rely less on others for your fun.

4. Write down your feelings.

Finally, it can become extremely overwhelming to keep all your negative thoughts locked up in your mind. One technique to help rid you of negative thoughts is to write them down and read them out loud. Sometimes this technique can make you realize how silly they are. On top of that, there is something therapeutic about writing down your thoughts and bringing them out of your mind and onto paper. When you are done, you can rip up the paper and throw it in the bin, along with those pesky negative thoughts.

Chapter 5: Communicating With Your Partner and Designing the Future Together

Communication problems are not uncommon, and they often crop up from time to time in most romantic relationships. While some conversations can be tough to have, talking about your fears and anxieties is the best way to move forward and help address those issues.

Without communication, you are left to mull over your fears on your own, which can lead to further anxiety issues and false assumptions. This can lead to a relationship that becomes based on distrust, fear, and jealousy—things that should not be present in a happy and healthy relationship.

This is why communication is such an essential part of any relationship—it is often the most influential factor that causes different anxiety issues.

Did Communication With Your Partner Die Down After Marriage?

When it comes to marriage issues, communication is often the root cause of a lot of them, and it can easily be lost if you do not continue to work on it with your partner. Some couples think that they no longer need to work on their relationship once they are married. But that couldn't be further from the truth!

Once married, it is easy to slip into bad habits of going through the motions and not discussing your thoughts and feelings with your significant other. If they are also doing the same, then this can cause issues further down the line. Issues such as anxiety caused by not knowing where you stand, sex life differences, stress, lack of money, and loss of trust do not just go away once you are married.

If you lose your communication skills in marriage, these issues can rear their ugly heads again and wreak havoc in your relationship.

All these issues stem from not discussing how you feel with your partner, which is why you must keep communication high even after getting married. Don't worry, though; there are many ways you can take to improve your communication or bring it back to the level before marriage.

Reliable Ways to Share Stress With Your Partner

One of the main aspects of being in a relationship is supporting each other with issues and experiencing things together. One issue that most humans deal with at some point in their life is stress. There are some ways you can share your stress as a couple.

1. Notice symptoms of stress. Make sure you are looking out for stress-related symptoms in your partner. It may be that they are too shy to say anything or aren't even aware of the symptoms themselves, so it's essential to keep an eye on anything out of the ordinary. This will put you in an excellent position to tackle the issue when you bring it up or when your partner comes to you for help.

2. Talk to your partner. Communication is one of the best ways to deal with stress. Stress cannot be managed well if you won't share your thoughts with your partner. By saying out loud what is stressing you, some of the stress will be lifted. You also put yourself in a position to discuss it in more detail with your partner for them to help you through it.

3. Listen. If your partner comes to you with issues surrounding stress, it is essential that you are ready and prepared to listen. Ensure you pay close attention to what they are saying. Let them get it all off their chest before contributing, and ensure you don't belittle how they are feeling with the language you use.

4. Comfort. Aside from not belittling them, it is also vital that you comfort your partner. Make sure that you reassure them whenever you can. The first stage of helping a partner with stress is assuring them that it is okay and that you will work through the issues they have together as a team.

5. Become active. Once you have established a level of comfort, there is no greater remedy for stress than exercise! Plan a walk, exercise at home, or hit the gym together. You will immediately feel better as your body physically deals with the stress and your mind is elsewhere for a significant period.

6. Make a list. If exercise isn't your thing, make a list of things you love to do as a couple to combat stress. You should make this list together so that you and your partner can contribute to what is written down. You will start to feel some stress release even by just making this list.

Talking About Sex With Your Partner

This one can be tricky. Often people feel anxious about bringing up the subject of sex with their partner, as they fear it may lead to their partner feeling angry or embarrassed, and it could end the relationship. Ultimately, if you are unhappy with your sex life, it is likely the relationship will end anyway. So when you think about it that way, you've got nothing to lose!

1. Start early. It's good to discuss your sex life with your partner early on in the relationship. Having these conversations early allows you to establish ground rules in advance. It also builds up another layer of trust that other parts of your relationship can grow from. If you leave it too long, it will become more and more challenging to start the conversation.

2. Or start as soon as possible. It is never too late. Even if you have been with your partner for a long time, you can still broach the subject, and the elements such as increased trust and understanding will always be prevalent.

3. Discuss fantasies. Telling anyone your deepest fantasies can be tricky. For some reason, despite being something we know we will find pleasure from, we find it embarrassing to discuss these with our significant other. However, it is crucial to do so to ensure you are getting everything you desire out of your sexual relationship with your partner.

3. Pick the right time. Although it is vital to act fast, there is a time and place to have these conversations! For example, it's probably not a conversation you want to begin when you are having dinner with your partner's parents! Finding the right time is important, as it will allow you to discuss in a safe and private place to get genuinely intimate.

*4. **Take ownership.*** Take your sexual pleasure into your own hands! If you want your partner to try something that you know you will enjoy, then tell them! You should be able to discuss any fantasies with your partner, knowing that the conversation is between the two of you and that they will be attentive and listen to your needs.

*5. **Be clear.*** Be clear about what it is you want that you aren't currently getting. These conversations can come as a surprise to your significant other, so it's important you make the details easy to follow and digest.

*6. **Be positive.*** It's also essential to be positive with your partner. You don't want to hurt their feelings by telling them they are doing something wrong. Instead, focus on some of the things they do that you love while also including things you would like them to try more of.

*7. **Listen.*** Finally, make sure you are ready to listen to your partner. You may be surprised to hear that your partner also has fantasies and things that they would like to do more or less off. Make sure you are ready to not only explain your thoughts but also be receptive to your partners.

Approaches to Seduce and Flirt With Your Partner

Flirting is often seen as something only single people or those in a new relationship do, but that is not the case! You can still seduce and flirt with your partner even when you've been married or in a relationship for a long time already. Here are some ways to do it:

*1. **Offer compliments in private.*** One way to keep up the romance in your relationship is to compliment your partner. Over time, it is easy to assume that your partner knows you think they look beautiful, but that isn't necessarily the case. Throwing a compliment out there now and then goes a long way and, if nothing else, will put a smile on their face. Make sure the compliment is genuine, though. No one likes a faker!

2. Offer compliments in public. Don't think that compliments should just be in private. By telling your partner how much you value them and complimenting them in public, you are showing them that you are proud and feel honored to be seen with them. This one depends on your partner's likes, though, as it can make some people feel uncomfortable and shy.

3. Dress up for each other. Make an effort! Once a couple has been together for a long time, it can be easy to turn up in your joggers and lounge around on the couch. Spice it up a little by dressing up smartly and going out for a nice meal or dance. This will make you both feel great about yourself and each other, adding more romance to your relationship.

4. Get touchy-feely. Within reason, of course! When in the comfort of your own home and with your partner's consent, there is no reason not to get a little handsy. Little touches of affection are a great physical way of showing your partner that you care. It makes them feel welcome and attractive. Run your hand through their hair. Kiss their neck. It's the little things that make the most difference.

5. Get sexting. It's 2020. Get on your phone and get sexting. Send your partner a cheeky message while they are at work, or build up a sexual fantasy over mobiles before you see each other. Just bear in mind that you have to be careful when sending anything explicit. The internet is for life, so don't put anything out there that you would potentially be embarrassed by in the future.

6. Innuendo is still the king. A nice and easy one here—don't pass up the opportunity to slip in a little innuendo! Again, this isn't suitable for all conversations or locations, but a little innuendo here and there can go a long way.

Conclusion

In summary, it is worth remembering that you are not the only one who is dealing with relationship anxiety. Millions of people across the world are going through similar issues. You are just one step closer to resolving them as you have taken the time to research and read this book for tips and advice!

If you take one thing from this book, it is that communication is the cornerstone of dealing with any relationship anxiety. Talking does make everything better! It is vital for any relationship at any stage to have mature and calm conversations about how you are feeling. It helps you reach amicable conclusions about how you are going to proceed.

Whether you are in a new relationship discussing issues of trust and fear of abandonment or in a long-term relationship talking about a lack of communication or libido, these conversations are all vital. They will make a huge difference when it comes to dealing with anxiety in relationships.

If You Enjoyed This Book in Anyway, an Honest Review Is Always Appreciated!